Abcs

for Special Children:
Red on Black, Yellow on Black

Erin Fulks © 2019
Book 2

Sometimes it is challenging to find learning tools for our special children. My books are meant to help children who are visually impaired learn basic to complicated object patterns. Through my studies of various conditions and diseases, I have learned that many visually impaired persons can see simple colors with simple backgrounds. Many visually impaired persons see well red objects on a black background the best. While others see yellow objects on black background better.

These are picture books with no words as to allow the caregiver to add words in their language if desired. If you have any suggestions for books you would like made for your child, please contact the author at erin@achievemilestones.com.

Please note that you are welcome to use these books with any child, not just the visually impaired.

b

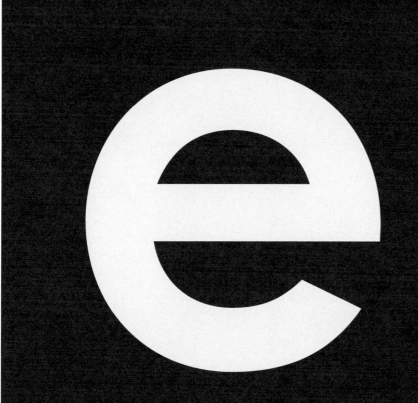

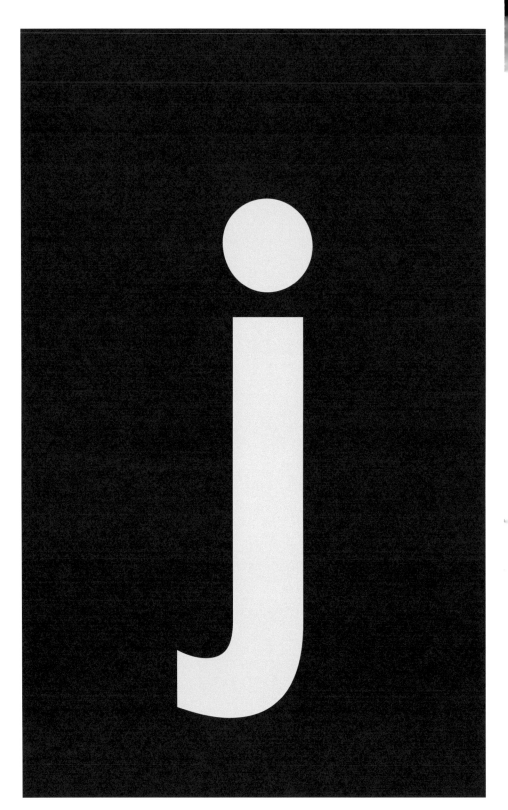

m

p

W

CVI APPAREL

www.achivemilestones.com
Click on "Apparel"
Click on "CVI Apparel"
Click on "Education"

Adult Capital ABC Shirt

Adult Lowercase ABC Shirt

Adult Awareness Shirt

**Adult Awareness Shirt
With Ribbon**

Request Custom Apparel : erin@achievemilestones.com

Book 1

Other Books by This Author

Animals for Children With CVI: Red on Black,
Yellow on Black, White on Black

Animals for Children With CVI: Red on White,
Yellow on White, Black on White

ABCs for Special Children:
Yellow on Black, Red on Black

ABCs for Special Children:
Yellow on White, Red on White

ABCs for Special Children:
Red on Black, White on Black

ABCs for Special Children:
Red on White, Black on White

ABCs for Special Children:
Yellow on Black, White on Black

ABCs for Special Children:
Yellow on White, Black on White

ABCs for Special Children:
Purple on Black, Green on Black

ABCs for Special Children:
Purple on White, Green on White

ABCs for Special Children:
Blue on White, Orange on White

ABCs for Special Children:
Blue on Black, Orange on Black

Colors for Special Children:
Black Background

Colors for Special Children:
White Background

Shapes for Special Children:
Red on Black, Yellow on Black, White on Black

Shapes for Special Children:
Red on White, Yellow on White, Black on White

Numbers for Special Children:
Red on Black, Yellow on Black, White on Black

Numbers for Special Children:
Red on White, Yellow on White, Black on White

Shapes and Numbers for Special Children:
Red on Black, 1-10

Shapes and Numbers for Special Children:
Red on White, 1-10

Shapes and Numbers for Special Children:
Yellow on Black,1-10

Shapes and Numbers for Special Children:
Yellow on White, 1-10

Shapes and Numbers for Special Children:
Red on Black, 11-20

Shapes and Numbers for Special Children:
Red on White, 11-20

Shapes and Numbers for Special Children:
Yellow on Black, 11-20

Shapes and Numbers for Special Children:
Yellow on White, 11-20

Learning the Body for Special Children:
Red on Black, Yellow on Black

Learning the Body for Special Children:
Red on White, Yellow on White

Christmas for Special Children:
Red on Black

Christmas for Special Children:
Red on White

Christmas for Special Children:
Yellow on Black

Christmas for Special Children:
Yellow on White

Shapes and Colors for Special Children:
Red on Black

Shapes and Colors for Special Children:
Red on White

Shapes and Colors for Special Children:
Yellow on Black

Shapes and Colors for Special Children:
Yellow on White

Numbers for Special Children:
Red on Black 1-100

Numbers for Special Children:
Yellow on Black 1-100

Where to find these books:

Printed Versions: Amazon
$21.99 - $25.99 each

Kindle Versions: Amazon - If Available
$7.99 each

Downloadable eBooks: www.achievemilestones.com
$4.99 each

I hope your child enjoys any variety of the books I have written. Your special child is my inspiration.

It is my goal to create awareness for various types of conditions and diseases, not just the visually impaired. Except for book sales, all the profit from products on my website, www.achievemilestones.com, is donated to charities specific to the condition or disease the product's sponsor.

My child is alive because of generous donors to foundations like CureSMA. A drug that stopped the progression of my daughter's disease was FDA approved just days before her birth. I had a prayer answered before I even knew I needed a miracle. My greatest desire is for your child's condition or disease to have a cure like mine did. I am doing this by giving to foundations whose sole purpose is this.

My best to your child's success,

Erin Fulks

Made in United States
Troutdale, OR
11/26/2023

14984887R00036